LIVERPOOL TRAMWAYS

Brian P Martin
Series editor Robert J Harley

2. The Southern Routes

MP Middleton Press

Cover Picture: The sylvan nature of South Liverpool is typified by the reserved tracks at Allerton Road in Woolton. More is revealed in picture 96.

Cover Colours: Red and cream livery was inaugurated by manager C.R.Bellamy and carried on by succeeding managers, C.W.Mallins and Percy Priestly. Although the green livery was heralded by the Priestly Bogies in 1933, cars in the old red livery could still be seen in service as late as 1949.

To Peter and Madeleine (my son and daughter-in-law) and my grandchildren Alexandra and Hollyanne, who lived for a short while in Woolton, South Liverpool.

Published September 1998

ISBN 1 901706 23 0

© *Middleton Press, 1998*

Design Deborah Goodridge

Published by
Middleton Press
Easebourne Lane
Midhurst, West Sussex
GU29 9AZ
Tel: 01730 813169
Fax: 01730 812601

Printed & bound by Biddles Ltd,
Guildford and Kings Lynn

CONTENTS

INTRODUCTION AND ACKNOWLEDGEMENTS

Interest in Liverpool trams is still very much a going concern with three active local tram societies and the heritage line at Birkenhead where Liverpool trams can be seen. It is over forty years since the last tram ran in Liverpool and it is pretty safe to say that the "Green Goddess" is still remembered and revered with affection by generations of Liverpudlians. Following on from *Vol. 1: The Eastern Routes*, this second volume of *Tramway Classics* deals with the routes of the south end of the city. A third volume will concentrate on the routes of Liverpool's north end and finally a fourth will delve into the various cross city services which linked the north and the south.

This volume depicts the routes on the main corridors of Wavertree Road, Smithdown Road, Princes Park, Park Road, Aigburth Road, Menlove Avenue and Mather Avenue. The peak hour routes 32 and 38 are also covered.

My thanks go to those whose photographs appear in this volume: R.B.Parr, H.B.Priestley and N.N.Forbes whose collections are now part of the National Tramway Museum records, R.Dudley-Caton, Merseyside Tramway Preservation Society, Wallasey Tramcar Preservation Group, J.W.Gahan, E.A.Gahan, R.J.S.Wiseman, A.D.Packer, R.Stephens, R.Anderson, R.W.A.Jones, R.G.Hemshall, T.A.Packwood, D.Tate, A.C.Noon Collection, A.S.Clayton, K.G.Harvie, R.Brook, Liverpool City Engineers, the late E.R.Vaughan, Martin Jenkins, D.A.Thompson, S.Watkins, G.H.F.Atkins, the late J.H.Roberts, J.Clough, Liverpool Corporation Passenger Transport, W.J.Wyse and the South Liverpool Weekly News. Apologies to those whose pictures I have not been able to identify - these are entered as part of my own collection.

I am eternally grateful to Tom Murphy for his photographic help and to Steve Molloy for rescuing old rare paper negatives on his Apple computer. Thanks are due to Harry Moore, Ted Gahan and Geoff Price for allowing me access to their collections. Sincere thanks to Jack Gahan - the highest authority on Liverpool trams - for always answering my infinite queries and to Tony Gahan for painstakingly reading the manuscript. My gratitude also goes to Harry Moore, a south end man, for his advice and suggestions. I am also indebted to Leo Taylor for the use of his excellent rolling stock plans.

The 1927 Ordnance Survey maps were supplied by the Liverpool Central Libraries Record Office and have north at the top unless shown otherwise. The map of the south end routes is by courtesy of Terry Daniel and depot sketches are reproduced by permission of Bruce Maund from *Liverpool Transport*. The system map and list of tram routes are from the LCPT Transport Guide for 1947. The actual size photocopies of staff cap badges are from Geoff Price's collection and reproduced with his permission.

May I commend readers who wish to know more about Liverpool trams to read *Liverpool Transport* by J.B.Horne and T.B.Maund, *Edge Lane Roundabout* by B.P.Martin, *A Nostalgic Look at Liverpool Trams 1945-57* by S.Palmer and B.P.Martin, *Liverpool Tramways 1943-57* by R.E.Blackburn, *Liverpool Trams Fleet List* by T.J.Martin and the many volumes of pocket picture albums on Liverpool Trams published by the MTPS by T.J.Martin. Especially about trams in the south end: *By Tram to Garston* by the late Eric Vaughan.

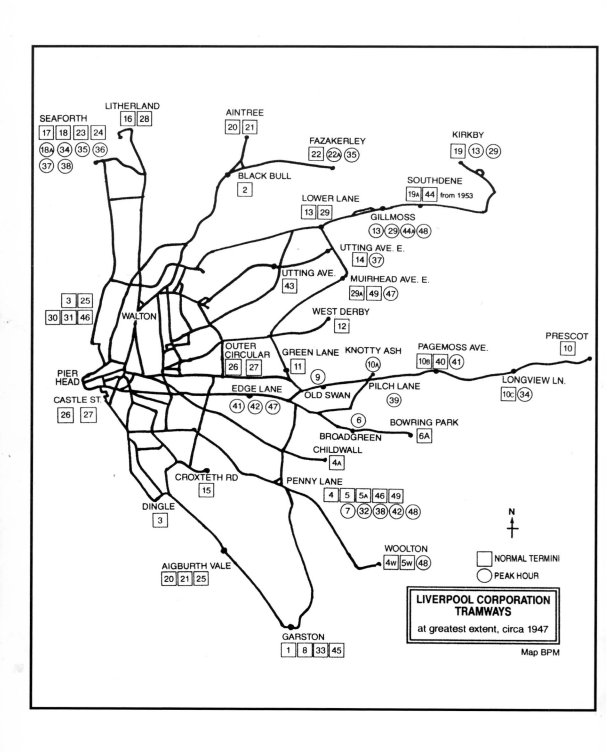

LITHERLAND
16 28

SEAFORTH
17 18 23 24
18A 34 35 36
37 38

AINTREE
20 21

FAZAKERLEY
22 22A 35

KIRKBY
19 13 29

BLACK BULL
2

LOWER LANE
13 29

SOUTHDENE
19A 44 from 1953

GILLMOSS
13 29 44A 48

UTTING AVE. E.
14 37

UTTING AVE.
43

MUIRHEAD AVE. E.
29A 49 47

WEST DERBY
12

3 25
30 31 46

WALTON

OUTER
CIRCULAR
26 27

GREEN LANE
11

KNOTTY ASH
10A

PAGEMOSS AVE.
10B 40 41

PRESCOT
10

PIER
HEAD

EDGE LANE
41 42 47

9

OLD SWAN

PILCH LANE
39

LONGVIEW LN.
10C 34

CASTLE ST.
26 27

6

BROADGREEN

BOWRING PARK
6A

CHILDWALL
4A

CROXTETH RD
15

PENNY LANE
4 5 5A 46 49
7 32 38 42 48

DINGLE
3

WOOLTON
4W 5W 48

NORMAL TERMINI
PEAK HOUR

AIGBURTH VALE
20 21 25

N

**LIVERPOOL CORPORATION
TRAMWAYS**

at greatest extent, circa 1947

Map BPM

GARSTON
1 8 33 45

GEOGRAPHICAL SETTING

Liverpool stands on the east bank of the River Mersey at its mouth, where it joins the expanse of Liverpool Bay and the Irish Sea. Formerly in Lancashire, although its cosmopolitan nature belied this fact, yet the so obvious Lancashire towns of Southport, Ormskirk, Prescot, St. Helens, Warrington and Widnes closely surround Liverpool. Now it is in the county of Merseyside.

HISTORICAL BACKGROUND

The antiquity of Liverpool goes back to Saxon times, although there is nothing existing of its most ancient buildings - the tower and the castle - on the site of which now stands the Victoria Monument. The oldest building, the Bluecoat Chambers, dates back to 1717. The first event of local importance was on 28th August 1207, when King John granted a charter creating Liverpool a free borough. Previously only a fishing village, a second charter granted by Henry III in 1229 conferred rights upon merchants the privileges of buying and selling of merchandise and of electing their own mayor, sheriffs and bailiffs.

It was not until the opening up of the New World that Liverpool's pre-eminence as an Atlantic port was established. The iniquitous triangular slave trade with America and West Africa undoubtedly contributed vastly to Liverpool's wealth. The extension of the docks system in the 19th century, both northwards and southwards of the Pier Head created a need for public transport. The opening of the Liverpool and Manchester Railway (the world's first passenger line) in 1830 also created a new demand and pattern of requirements. Stagecoaches and horse buses served the docks and acted as feeders to the railway stations.

History decrees that it was Birkenhead which witnessed the first British street tramway in August 1860. Trams first appeared in Liverpool from the borough boundary at Fairfield to the Old Swan on 2nd July 1861. It was hoped to extend citywards as the line became accepted by its many critics and doubters. However, the track was removed by 1862. Despite this setback, the idea of smooth running horse trams was kept alive and in 1865 the Liverpool Tramways Co. was formed, but after laying a sample stretch of "non-obstructive" tramway in Castle Street, the company foundered legally and was dissolved. A new 1868 company was begun and by 1869 lines to Dingle and an Inner Circle were laid, the first cars running on 1st November. The horse tramways were gradually extended until they were superseded by the first electric cars. The Liverpool Tramways Co. was acquired by Liverpool Corporation in 1897 and soon set about electrifying the system, the first electric cars running a year later.

The city's first electric trams were German built Altona and Ringbahn single-deckers with matching trailers. These opened the electric services to Dingle. The second tramway to Princes Park Gates in 1899 utilised American-built, single deck, bogie cars known as "Philadelphias". By 1902 all the horse routes had been electrified, except for the disputed Litherland service which lingered on until August 1903.

Various derivatives of open-top four wheelers built by the blossoming British tram builders, Milnes, Westinghouse and Dick, Kerr, were put into service after the early demise of the vastly unsuitable German cars. The Preston type three-window car became standard and later received various top covers to develop as the famous Liverpool Bellamy cars - part of the tramway scene in the city for over a quarter of a century. Enclosed cars followed, which resulted in the superb series of the 1930s when the city's tramways were modernised, culminating in the development of the ultimate Liverpool tramcar, the finely designed bogie Streamliners of 1936. The four-wheel economy version of these, the Baby Grands, lasted until the end of tramway operation. In 1953-54 a total of 46 redundant Streamliners were sold to Glasgow and ran there until 1960.

Liverpool's tram routes at their zenith totalled 97 route miles of which 28 miles were on reserved tracks. The tram to bus conversion programme began in June 1948 with the closure of the 26/27 Outer Circular routes. Just over nine years later the city's last tram on the 6A and 40 routes ran on 14th September 1957.

In this volume the routes covered are:

No.	inward/north	outward /south
1	City	Garston and Penny Lane via Park Road
1A, 1B	"	Garston via Aigburth and Park Road
4	"	Wavertree/Penny Lane via Wavertree
4A	"	Childwall via Wavertree Road
4W	"	Woolton via Wavertree Road
5	"	Penny Lane/Wavertree via Smithdown Road
5A	"	Penny Lane only via Smithdown Road
5W	"	Woolton via Smithdown Road
7	"	Penny Lane (earlier Calderstones) via Smithdown Road
8	"	Aigburth and Garston via Smithdown Road
8A	"	Garston only via Smithdown Rd
15	"	Croxteth Road via Princes Road
32	"	Penny Lane via Park Lane and Smithdown Road
33	"	Garston via Princes Road an Aigburth
38	Seaforth	Penny Lane (postwar industrial service)
45	City	Garston via Mill Street and Aigburth
45A	"	Garston via Mill Street and Aigburth

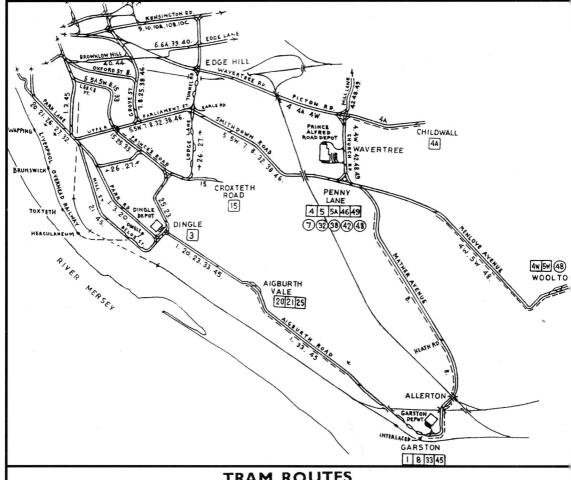

TRAM ROUTES

1	PENNY LANE & CITY via Garston & Aigburth
1A, 1B	GARSTON & CITY via Aigburth
*2	BLACK BULL & CITY via Walton
3	WALTON & DINGLE via Lime Street
4	PENNY LANE & CITY via Wavertree
4A	CHILDWALL & CITY via Wavertree
4W	WOOLTON & CITY via Wavertree
5	WAVERTREE & CITY via Smithdown Road
5A	PENNY LANE & CITY via Smithdown Road
5W	WOOLTON & CITY via Smithdown Road
6	BROADGREEN & CITY via Edge Lane
6A	BOWRING PARK & CITY via Edge Lane
*7	PENNY LANE & CITY via London Road
8	AIGBURTH & CITY via Garston & Smithdown Road
8A	GARSTON & CITY via Smithdown Road
*9	OLD SWAN & CITY via Kensington
10	PRESCOT & CITY via Old Swan
*10A	KNOTTY ASH & CITY via Old Swan
10B	PAGEMOSS AVENUE & CITY via Old Swan
10C	LONGVIEW LANE & CITY via Old Swan
11	GREEN LANE & CITY via Tuebrook
12	WEST DERBY & CITY via Tuebrook
13	EAST LANCS. ROAD & CITY via Townsend Lane
13A	BROAD LANE & CITY via Townsend Lane
14	UTTING AVENUE EAST & CITY via Townsend Lane
*14A	CHERRY LANE & CITY via Townsend Lane
15, 15A	CROXTETH ROAD & CITY via Princes Park
16	LITHERLAND & CITY via Vauxhall Road
17	SEAFORTH & CITY via Derby Road
18	SEAFORTH & BRECKFIELD RD. via Everton Valley
*18A	SEAFORTH & EVERTON RD. via Everton Valley
19	KIRKBY, HORN HOUSE LANE or GILLMOSS & CITY via Robson Street
19A	LOWER LANE & CITY via Robson Street
20	AINTREE & AIGBURTH via Park Road (short journeys 20A)
21	AINTREE & AIGBURTH via Mill Street
22	FAZAKERLEY & CITY via Walton Road
*22A	FAZAKERLEY & CITY via Hale Road
23	SEAFORTH & CITY via Strand Road
24	SEAFORTH & CITY via Knowsley Road
25	WALTON & AIGBURTH via Moss Street
26	OUTER CIRCULAR via Oakfield Rd. & Lodge Lane (short journeys 26A)
27	OUTER CIRCULAR via Lodge Lane & Oakfield Rd (short journeys 27A)
28	LITHERLAND & CITY via Scotland Road
29	EAST LANCASHIRE ROAD & CITY via Tuebrook
29A	MUIRHEAD AVENUE EAST & CITY via Tuebrook
30	WALTON & CITY via Netherfield Road
31	WALTON & CITY via Heyworth Street
*32	PENNY LANE & CITY via Park Lane
33	GARSTON & CITY via Princes Park
*34	LONGVIEW LANE & SEAFORTH via Everton Valley
*35	FAZAKERLEY & SEAFORTH via Hale Road
*36	LOWER LANE & SEAFORTH via Hale Road
*37	UTTING AV. EAST & SEAFORTH via Everton Valley
*38	PENNY LANE & SEAFORTH via Heyworth Street
*39	KNOTTY ASH & CITY via Brookside Avenue
40	PAGEMOSS AVENUE & CITY via Brookside Ave.
*41	PAGEMOSS AVENUE & CITY via Old Swan
*42	PENNY LANE & EDGE LANE via Mill Lane
43, 43B	UTTING AVENUE & CITY via Everton Valley
*43A	UTTING AVENUE & CITY via Robson Street
44	KIRKBY or GILLMOSS & CITY via Everton Valley
44A	LOWER LANE & CITY via Everton Valley
45	PENNY LANE & CITY via Aigburth & Mill Street
45A	GARSTON & CITY via Aigburth & Mill Street
46	PENNY LANE & WALTON via Moss Street
*47	MUIRHEAD AVE. EAST & EDGE LANE
*48	PENNY LANE & GILLMOSS or MUIRHEAD AVENUE EAST & WOOLTON
49	PENNY LANE & MUIRHEAD AVE. EAST via Old Swan
	DINGLE & GILLMOSS

*Denotes Part-time Routes

*CAIRO ST. & PAGEMOSS
(see Vol-1; caption photo! 65)

CITY TO DINGLE (VIA PARK ROAD)

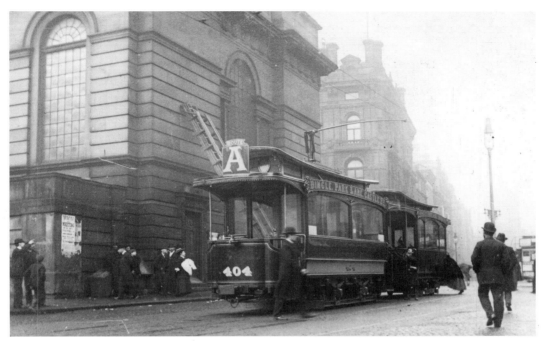

1. Liverpool's first electric route was service A from Castle Street to Dingle via Park Lane and Park Road. Pictured is one of the German motor cars and trailers which inaugurated the service. The church on the left is St. George's, which was demolished to make way for the Queen Victoria Monument. Just behind, on the corner of Castle Street, is the former bank which today is known as Trials Hotel because of its proximity to the QE II Law Courts. (A.C.Noon Coll.)

2. Soon a second route - B to Princes Park Gates - was in operation utilising the second series of electric cars, the Philadelphia's, which were imported from the USA. St George's Crescent is in the background with Lord Street to the right, as cars on lines A and B reverse for their journeys back to the south end. (B.P.Martin Coll.)

3. A close-up shows a Philadelphia car at Castle Street terminus. Note the young "tramway boy" alongside car 441. His function was to change the points with an iron bar. In 1904 the boys gained the privilege of a "servants pass" to get to and from work. Many of these boys went on to become conductors and motormen. (A.C.Noon Coll.)

→

4. Priestly car 683 is seen in Lord street at the North John Street junction; it is travelling to the Pier Head in 1932, and is followed by a Bellamy car. Note the Armstrong Siddeley motor car and a Crosville bus alongside. Thos Cook's travel bureau still occupies premises at this end of Lord Street. (R.B.Parr)

5. Lord Street features the famous Bunney's Corner at the Whitechapel junction which today is occupied by Barratt's, with MacDonalds, Mothercare and Next making up the other corners. Car 126, an open top Preston type, car 133, a Little Emma, and Bellamy car 481 represent the mainstay of the fleet in the year 1908. (A.C.Noon Coll.)

6. A Priestly 1924 car with extended vestibule is observed at the Pier Head in 1949 on a peak hour 1B service to Aigburth Vale only. Car 638 was modernised in April 1936 and was in service until 20th June 1950. (A.S.Clayton)

7. Bogie Streamliner car 951 is loading passengers on a Clayton Square extra on route 1 on 15th July 1947. The bulk of Lime Street Station provides a background for the Crown Hotel on the Lime Street/Skelhorne Street corner. Wills Capstan cigarettes advert dominates the scene in Elliott Street with the old St John's Market on the corner of Gt Charlotte Street. (B.P.Martin Coll.)

8. Priestly wide vestibule car 652 on a peak hour 1A to Garston is seen in Berry Street in 1949 from the steps of St Luke's Church, which was bombed in the Second World War and remains today as a ruin and monument to man's folly. One of Blackler's temporary Bold Street shops is on the left corner, whilst the distinctive round tower of what is today Rapid Hardware Stores adorns the corner of Renshaw Street on the right. (E.A.Gahan)

9. War dishevelled car 881 heads for the city on a route 1 and crosses Duke Street into Berry Street. The bike shop, today a Chinese Restaurant, purveys Raleigh cycles and Sturmey Archer gears! Note the distinctive tower on the building which still survives today. (N.N.Forbes)

10. Liverpool's only single decker, car 757, passes the Ancient Chapel of Toxteth and is beginning to take the curve to Dingle Depot. On the left was Dingle Station, the Liverpool Overhead Railway's southern terminal - an underground section on an overhead railway! This experimental single decker was designed for multiple unit operation under the Mersey Tunnel to Birkenhead and/or on a subway route to Everton. Both farsighted schemes came to nought and car 757 only saw service from 1929 to 1935. (B.P.Martin Coll.)

11. Pictured outside the original part of Dingle Depot, Bellamy car 506 on the 1 to Garston disgorges its passengers. In service in 1908 this tram, a former First Class car, was withdrawn from passenger service in December 1942 to become a snowplough. It succumbed in the disastrous Green Lane Depot fire of November 1947, when 66 trams were lost. Dingle Depot was enlarged and reconstructed in 1937. (B.P.Martin Coll.)

Dingle car sheds in 1927 and before the Mill Street extension.

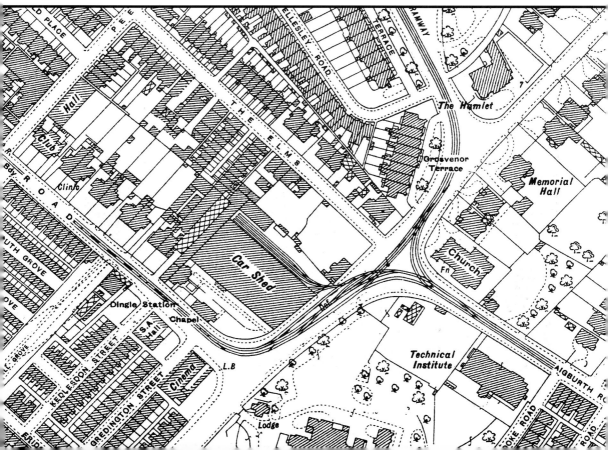

CITY TO DINGLE (VIA MILL STREET)

12. Tram route 45 ran to Garston via Mill Street. Opened in 1927, it proved successful in adding to the service to serve the burgeoning extensions of property in the south end. Car 696, a Priestly wide vestibule car with the large indicators (compare with the small type in Picture 6), is seen at the Pier Head keeping company with car 870 on route 8. Car 696 is standing on the Garston siding, Liverpool's last extension, constructed in 1946.   (N.N.Forbes)

13. We observe a busy last day scene on routes 45 and 45A at Castle Street/Victoria Monument in September 1951. The 45 originally traversed Renshaw Street, but was altered to run via Park Lane and South Castle Street in August 1949. To alleviate temporarily the effects of other tramway abandonments and shortage of buses, an all day 45A service was inaugurated between Aigburth Vale and South Castle Street via Mill Street in August 1951. By the September all trams on route 45 had been replaced by buses. Here cars 958 and 951 circumnavigate the Victoria Monument. (A.S.Clayton)

14. On the last day of operation, car 958 is seen again, this time at the South Castle Street/Canning Place corner, where trams ran round three sides of the war damaged Custom House to gain access to Park Lane and the south end. It is a shame the Custom House was not restored, instead it was demolished eventually in favour of an anonymous modern glass fronted building. With bombed sites behind, the remaining buildings include Sewill's Nautical Horologists, still trading today, and on the first floor H. Poll, Tailor. (N.N.Forbes)

15. With South John Street in the background, car 951, on a 45A bound for Aigburth, rounds the eastern side of the old Custom House on the widely spaced tracks at Canning Place, where Steers House (now due for demolition) still stands, near to the present day Merseyside Police HQ. The year is 1951, the last year of tram operation. (N.N.Forbes)

16. Route 45 trams traversed Mill Street, past the flour mills near Grain Street and Corn Street and through a network of streets known locally as the "Holy Land" - Moses Street, Isaac Street, Jacob Street and David Street, until coming to Parkhill Road. In the picture car 925, a Maley & Taunton trucked bogie Streamliner, is seen at the Parkhill Road junction with Beloe Street where the tracks, because of the narrow throughfare, were placed close together, thus precluding two cars passing. Note the signal lights on the pole on the left. To the right is a Blackledges bread shop, a local brand long disappeared.   (N.N.Forbes)

17. Another Maley, car 919, descends the sloping Beloe Street. The closeness of the tracks can be clearly seen. Although some of the properties are boarded up, it was more than a decade later before the road was widened. A last day scene of the 45, taken in September 1951. (A.S.Clayton)

18. Amidst the architectural splendour of the Royal Liver Building and the Cunard Building, a Priestly Standard awaits departure time from the Pier Head for Garston on route 33. Note the route card in the saloon window and the prefab windscreen with its canvas strip which allowed its loose bodywork to flex. A newly repainted car 762 (now preserved by the MTPS) is in front, also on the 33.   (B.P.Martin Coll.)

19. From the Pier Head terminal, south end bound cars sauntered round the curves of Mann Island which boxed the compass. This was the city terminal of Crosville bus routes to the east and south of Liverpool. A British Road Services lorry mingles with three Crosville vehicles, whilst a long bus queue awaits at the 82 stop with Voss Motors, Austin dealers, in the background, left. To the right, Liverpool's mighty Anglican Cathedral rears skywards.   (H.B.Priestley)

20. When Castle Street tram terminus became redundant and went over to buses, just one track round the Victoria Monument was retained for emergency use. Here 967 on a 33 working has been diverted and is seen gaining the outward tracks again in Derby Square and Lord Street. (Merseyside Tramway Preservation Society)

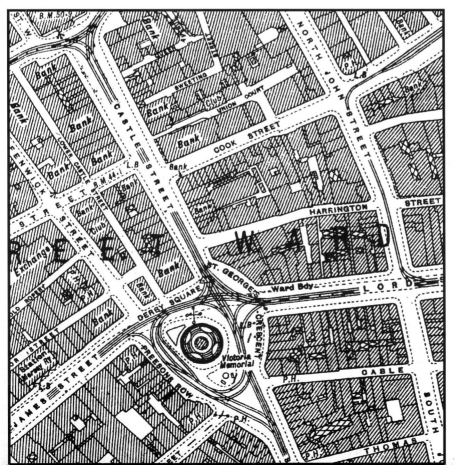

The Castle Street terminus around the Victoria Monument with the now vanished names of Preesons Row and St Georges Crescent, which commemorated the name of St George's church which once stood on the site of the monument.

21. Route 8 and 33 trams used the same tracks as far as the Rialto. Cars on route 8 then went via Upper Parliament Street, whilst the 33s traversed Princes Road. Car 874 on an 8A and car 936 on the 33 are seen on the Myrtle Street/Catharine Street corner with the old Children's Hospital in the left background. The former women's hospital was to the right. (K.G.Harvie)

22. A bit further on, Garston bound cars crossed Canning Street before reaching the Rialto. On the right is the Catholic Apostolic Church, destroyed by fire in 1985 and recently demolished. (K.G.Harvie)

23. Beyond the Rialto, route 33 trams traversed a single carriageway section before gaining the magnificent reserved tracks of Princes Road. Behind the tram is St Margaret's C of E Church and next to it the Princes Road Synagogue. The trams by now had to contend with new corporation Crossley buses running beyond the tram termini to Halewood and Speke. Here an 80C bus tries to overtake car 927 to beat it to the Rialto junction. (K.G.Harvie)

24. Car 962 is depicted on the Princes Road reserved tracks with one of the numerous Welsh churches in the city on the left, the Presbyterian Church of Wales, which it is claimed has the tallest spire in Liverpool. The Rialto is in the left distance. To the right, the grandeur of the former dwellings of prosperous merchants of the port of Liverpool, today mostly split into flats. (B.P.Martin Coll.)

26. Princes Park Gates is shown after the demise of the 15 and 27 routes which diverged left into Croxteth Road. Opportunity was taken to alter this road junction with a roundabout, which meant realignment of the outward 33 tram tracks. This was done in 1950 and saw use until the end of the Garston service in June 1953. Here car 931 eases from Devonshire Road at the new roundabout into Princes Road on the 26th August 1952. (R.D.Caton)

←

25. At the end of Princes Road was the point known as Princes Park Gates. Here route 33 trams turned right into the architectural splendour of Devonshire Road, whilst the 15 and 27 trams went left to Croxteth Road. Cabin car 789 is seen soon after entering service in 1934. The streamlined paint scheme was a novel idea, but was dropped at first repaints for a more sober livery. The Cabins advertised Electricity, a contrast to the next series of trams, the Marks Bogies, which exclusively praised Gas! (R.Brook)

LIVERPOOL CORPORATION
PASSENGER TRANSPORT

Published Quarterly January April July October
3D

OFFICIAL
TRAM & BUS GUIDE
No. 100   Oct./Dec. 1948

27. Rounding the bend in Devonshire Road, the tracks entered Belvidere Road amongst the many grand properties. Paved in tarmac, this section proved a joy to traverse by tram, being an example of Liverpool trackwork which was not typical! Two 33 trams during the last week of tram operation pass near Belvedere Girls School, with a Beardsmore taxi anxious to get past. (R.J.S.Wiseman)

28. Belvidere Road is seen at the Dingle end, as car 936 passes on a Clayton Square only extra on the route 33. (B.P.Martin Coll.)

DINGLE TO GARSTON (VIA AIGBURTH)

29. Car 183 pauses at the Dalmeny Street stop on Aigburth Road during the last year of trams. To the right is the ladies and children's outfitter, Florence Danks, still in business in the 1970s. Near this point was the Mayfair Cinema. (B.P.Martin Coll.)

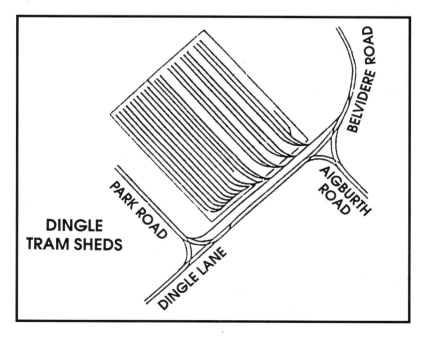

30. A classic view of Aigburth Vale reversing triangle was recorded in May 1899, with original German "Altona" motor cars and trailers; a "Ringbahn" set is behind on the first Liverpool electrified route A. The connecting horse bus for Garston awaits departure. This latter vehicle became superfluous when trams reached Garston in 1902, the Corporation in the meantime having absorbed the Garston & District Light Railway. (A.C.Noon Coll.)

31. The Vale became an important focal point on the Liverpool tram network, a terminus for several routes. It boasted a terminal siding and a trolley reverser. When photographed on 22nd April 1952 only the Garston circle was still tram operated. Car 925 is already showing 8 ready for its journey via Garston and back to the city via Mather Avenue. The photographer is looking towards the Dingle and citywards. (H.B.Priestley)

32. On the same day as the previous view, we are looking in the opposite direction, towards Garston, with the siding having rejoined the main line. Otterspool Park and Promenade to the right seem to be the destination of the lady with the plush pram, whilst a Ford Thames van belonging to Lunt's, another famous and now defunct, Liverpool bread firm, passes. (H.B.Priestley)

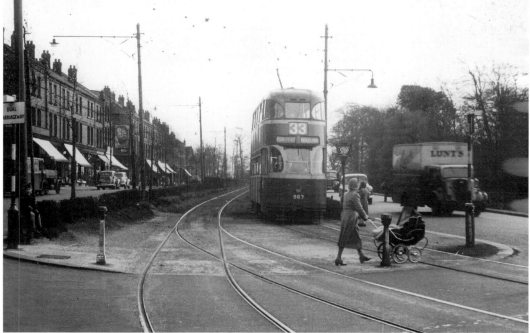

33. Beyond the Vale, the tracks to Garston included stretches of private right of way. Bellamy car 274, built in 1900 and in service until 1934, is seen at the Dundonald Road stop travelling inward on route 1. (Liverpool City Engineers/B.P.Martin Coll.)

34. Having just left the Riversdale Road stop at Liverpool Cricket Ground, car 928 is showing 8 on the blinds as it heads for Garston and the city via Mather Avenue. Taken on the last Friday of Garston Circle trams, 5th June 1953, there is just one more day in service for the trams to traverse these fine tracks. (R.J.S.Wiseman)

35. Approaching Garston, the reserved tracks gave way to street tracks. At Darby Grove on St Mary's Road there was a section of single track with passing loops at Dock Road, Moss Street and James Street with its length of interlaced track. In the 1970s a bypass was built at this point leaving the once busy St Mary's Road a mere backwater. (B.P.Martin Coll.)

36. Car 926, on the last Friday of tram operation, is rejoining the single section at the Dock Road loop, with the then, local Threlfalls Breweries Garston Hotel to the right. The shopping street of St Mary's Road stretches away behind. (H.B.Priestley)

37. Pictured on Moss Street loop, car 937 traverses the busy St Mary's Road intermingling with vans and Speke and City bound buses. A lady with a pram passes two others peering into Tyrer and Pendleton's jewellers window. (R.W.A.Jones)

38. The furthermost outward tracks of the south end routes were at Speke Road, where the tracks to Garston tram depot can be seen on the left. The picture is taken from the top deck of a tram which has just rounded the curve from St Mary's Road. The tracks can be seen in the left background heading back to the city. This link from Garston to Allerton via Horrocks Avenue and Woolton Road was opened in July 1939. The picture was taken during the first months of the war, on 6th April 1940. A future extension (but for the war) to Speke would have continued to the right. (H.B.Priestley)

39. Priestly Standard car 373 is pictured in Speke Road in 1937, before the link up with Allerton. The tracks were just a single stub, which continued into the depot. (H.B.Priestley)

40. A 1948 scene at the same point with car 694, one of the surviving red and cream liveried cars. A former open platform car, it is fitted with a "pre-fab" windscreen, complete with canvas strips to cover the dash rails. (E.A.Gahan)

41. Garston Depot's new extension featured just three tracks in the bus section. The original shed is to the right, and this housed five tracks. Two Maley & Taunton Streamliners await their turn of duty on the Garston Circle. (D.Tate)

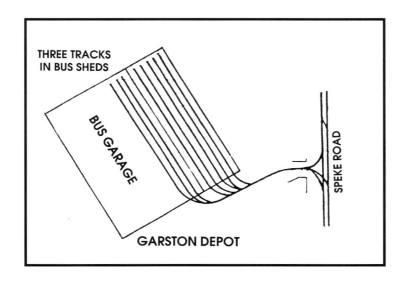

THREE TRACKS
IN BUS SHEDS

BUS GARAGE

GARSTON DEPOT

SPEKE ROAD

42. In 1908 a "super service" of trams was inaugurated, initially for a trial period on the Garston route. Seven cars were allotted and were finished in a livery of two shades of cream with elaborate gold, red and blue lining; they carried the legend FIRST CLASS on the stair stringers. These services were finally withdrawn in 1923. A total of 68 First Class cars were eventually provided on several routes. Most were Bellamys, but also included were two balcony cars and four Priestly Standards. Car 513 is seen outside Garston Depot in the early days of the service. (E.R. Vaughan Coll.)

43. In 1925 post boxes were affixed to certain cars leaving suburban terminals around 10 pm, Mondays to Fridays, for emptying on arrival in the city. This picture was a posed publicity shot to advertise the facility and shows a shawl clad "Mary Ellen" posting her letter with the real motorman looking on. (E.A.Gahan Coll.)

CITY TO CROXTETH ROAD (VIA PRINCES PARK)

44. An animated scene at the Pier Head south loop in 1947. Taking centre stage is Priestly Standard car 344 on the 15; this tram was built totally enclosed in 1931 at Edge Lane works. In front and behind is a bevy of Streamliners, one on the 8 and one on the 4. Is the dad (left) taking his daughter to New Brighton across the Mersey on the ferry? (B.P.Martin Coll.)

46. Lord Street in May 1949, with Priestly car 695 preceded by a Baby Grand bound for Woolton; a Marks Bogie follows on route 31 to Spellow Lane. The distinctive shop of Dunn & Co is on the corner of Doran's Lane - today the covered entrance to Cavern Walks, the "Beatles Area". Also occupying the building is the Liverpool Building Society later to be swallowed up by the Birmingham Midshires. (A.S.Clayton)

45. Pier Head - note the barn-like shelter, left, and looking towards the centre loop, we can see the wartime air-raid shelters. Car 143 has been fitted with the more substantial vestibule and has just received its first postwar repaint. The "Liverpool Corporation Passenger Transport" legend was discontinued soon after. Car 143 has not yet received its Liverpool coat of arms transfer. (D.A.Thompson)

47. Crossing the "Holy Junction" - Church Street/Lord Street/Whitechapel/Paradise Street - car 156 is seen travelling outwards towards Clayton Square. This vehicle was built in 1900 by Dick, Kerr, received its Bellamy top cover in 1904 and was finally withdrawn in 1936. Today this area is pedestrianised with HMV, W.H.Smith and C&A to the right, whilst River Island and Boots occupy the stores near where the famous Bunney's once stood. (B.P.Martin Coll.)

Routes 15, 15A.
CROXTETH ROAD—CITY.

STAGE No.		STAGE No.
IN	1½d. FARES (WORKMEN'S RETURN 2d.)	OUT
10	Croxteth Road and Upper Parliament Street...	5
11	North Hill Street and Hope Street	4
12	Upper Parliament Street and Renshaw Street (Upper Newington)	2
13	Renshaw Street (Upper Newington) and Pier Head	1
	2½d. FARE (WORKMEN'S RETURN 4d.)	
10	Croxteth Road and Renshaw Street (Upper Newington)	2
11	North Hill Street and Pier Head	1
	3d. FARE (WORKMEN'S RETURN 5d.)	
10	Croxteth Road and Pier Head	1

L.C.P.T.

48. Liverpool's famous Adelphi Hotel and Lewis's, one of the city's main stores (right) dominate Ranelagh Street, as Cabin car 810 newly in service allows pedestrians to cross over from Great Charlotte Street. (T.A.Packwood Coll.)

49. Ranelagh Place has the Adelphi Hotel (right) and the Vines Hotel to the right of Mallins Balcony car 478. The tram is about to turn left into Ranelagh Street. The ornately decorated tram shelter, complete with its decorative Liver Birds, can just be glimpsed to the right of the tram. (B.P.Martin Coll.)

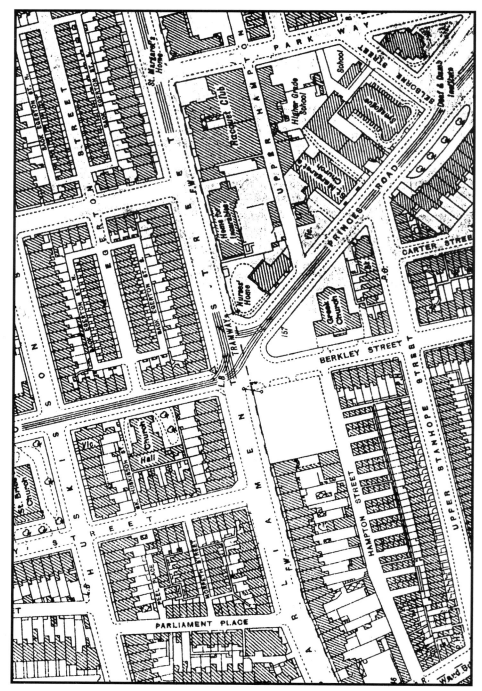

The Rialto Corner is at Upper Parliament Street, Princes Road and Catharine Street - also the junction of routes 8, 15, 25, 32, 33.

50. At Princes Park Gates, route 15 trams went left into Croxteth Road. Here in 1938 almost new bogie Streamliner car 947 takes on passengers at the superb tram shelter (which included a sub-station and an inspector's office) at the end of the Princes Road reservation. Worthy of note are the pre-war fashions and the fact that most people wore hats! (H.B.Priestley)

51. Cabin car 784 of 1933 has just passed the junction at Sefton Park Road, where Outer Circular cars on the 27 turned left, leaving the 15 route to continue for the short distance to the end of Croxteth Road at Ullet Road/Sefton Park. Indicators are already turned for the return journey back to the Pier Head. Note the skate on the overhead wire on the inward track, which operated the nearby traffic lights. Car 784 was the eventual last tram on the 15 route on 14th May 1949. (E.A.Gahan)

52. Sefton Park Road is to the left, the domain of 26 and 27 trams, whilst route 15 trams continued ahead. Streamliner car 944, barely over a year old, is seen on a fine August day in 1938. A Morris car of the period and a pick-up lorry wait at the lights. Although it is August, the man on the right wears his cap well pulled down as he carries his raincoat. (H.B.Priestley)

→

54. We observe the terminal stub with Streamliner car 967 ready for its Pier Head journey. Behind the tram to the left is Ullet Road; a mere half mile extension would have connected up with the Smithdown Road trams. To the right is Croxteth Gate, the entrance to the expansive Sefton Park. The tram entered service in March 1937 and was photographed just over a year later in May 1938. (H.B.Priestley)

53. Car 780, a Priestly Bogie, later demolished in a spectacular accident (see Vol. 3), waits for Priestly Standard car 26 to come off the reversing stub at the Croxteth Road terminus. A very "Liverpool" feature was the Picture Post advert where an eye was placed either side of the indicator. This advert was to be found only on Cabins, Marks and Priestly Bogies. It made the vehicles very "human" and in a way was an early form of Thomas the Tank Engine - for young passengers anyway! The church is the Sefton Park Presbyterian Church of England, demolished in the 1970s. (A.C.Noon Coll.)

The outer end of Princes Road at Princes Park Gates, with 15, 26, 27 routes to the left and 25 and 33 routes, right, into Devonshire Road.

CITY TO PENNY LANE (VIA WAVERTREE ROAD)

Routes 4, 4A, 4W.
WOOLTON—CHILDWALL—
WAVERTREE—CITY.

STAGE No. IN		STAGE No. OUT
	1½d. FARES (WORKMEN'S RETURN 2d.)	
4	Woolton and Yewtree Road · ...	10
5	Hillfoot Road and Cromptons Lane ...	9
6	Yewtree Road and Penny Lane ...	8
7	Cromptons Lane (4W) or Sefton Park Station (4) and Wavertree Clock Tower ...	7
8	Penny Lane (4 & 4W) or Childwall Five Ways (4A) and Ashfield ...	6
9	Wavertree Clock Tower and Durning Road ...	5
10	Ashfield and Edge Hill Church ...	4
11	Durning Road and Crown Street ...	3
12	Edge Hill Church and Lime Street ...	2
13	Lime Street and City Terminus ...	1
	2½d. FARES (WORKMEN'S RETURN 4d.)	
4	Woolton and Penny Lane ...	8
5	Hillfoot Road (4W) or Lodge Lane (4) and Wavertree Clock Tower ...	7
6	Yewtree Road (4W) or Portman Road (4) and Ashfield ...	6
7	Cromptons Lane (4W) or Sefton Park Station (4) and Durning Road ...	5
8	Penny Lane (4) or Childwall Five Ways (4A) and Edge Hill Church ...	4
9	Wavertree Clock Tower and Crown Street ...	3
10	Ashfield and Lime Street ...	2
11	Durning Road and City Terminus ...	1
	3d. FARES (WORKMEN'S RETURN 5d.)	
4	Woolton and Durning Road ...	5
10	Ashfield and City Terminus ...	1
	4d. FARES (WORKMEN'S RETURN 6d.)	
1	Woolton (4W) or Childwall Five Ways (4A) and City Terminus ...	1
OUT 3	Upper Parliament Street (Catharine Street) and Durning Road (via Church Road) ...	2

55. Car 440 was quite special - built in 1932 at Edge Lane as a Priestly Vestibule on a Brill type 8ft. 6ins/ 2592mm wheelbase trucks. It was modernised in 1935 as the pattern for future rebuilds and was then later fitted with an experimental Maley & Taunton 8ft./2440mm wheelbase four wheel truck. It received ventilators, large indicators and upholstered seats on both decks. Unfortunately, it was the slowest car in the fleet, but remained in service until July 1952. It is pictured at the Pier Head on route 4 to Penny Lane, keeping company with car 984 on route 1. (D.A.Thompson)

56. Liverpool's celebrity tram was Bellamy car 544, which outlasted all other members of its class in service by several years. It is reputed that depot staff hid it away when the transport committee made their inspections, in case they condemned it to the scrapyard. It was in excellent condition for its age - being built in 1910 and surviving until 1949, in service for an incredible total of 39 years! It is pictured at Old Haymarket on a peak hour extra on route 4. (J.W.Gahan)

57. At the site of one of Liverpool's "Grand Unions", where all sides of the Lime Street/ London Road/Commutation Row/William Brown Street junction were connected. One of the many imposing Liverpool branches of Burton's the Tailors can be seen in the background. Car 125, built in 1920 at Lambeth Road is an advance on the Bellamy type with its balcony top cover affording just a fraction more protection! (A.D.Packer)

58. When the Brownlow Hill tracks were laid in 1936, tram route 4A was inaugurated to serve newly extended tracks from Picton Clock, Wavertree, to Childwall Five Ways. Car 312, long-overdue for a repaint, is loading alongside the banqueting entrance of the Adelphi Hotel at the foot of Brownlow Hill in 1949. Here was one of the few single track sections on the Liverpool tramways. The clock of Parry's University Bookshop can just be discerned - a port of call for students heading for the University of Liverpool some two tramstops up the hill. (Wallasey Tramcar Preservation Group)

59. Just on the edge of the city, the topography of Liverpool becomes hilly, and with many narrow streets built in early days, single track one way systems were utilised. One such was Paddington inward, and Mount Vernon Road and Irvine Street outward. Here a Priestly Standard ascends Irvine Street at Holland Place. St Mary's, Edge Hill Church is to the right, whilst the tracks descending Paddington go off to the left. (N.N.Forbes)

60. After the gradual slope of Wavertree Road and crossing the Outer Circular (26, 27 routes) at Tunnel Road/Durning Road; the tracks then traversed Picton Road. Car 872 passes the Botanic House Hotel on the corner of Botanic Road, with Ridgeway Street and Eastwood Street in the background, before crossing over the Liverpool-London and Liverpool-Manchester railway at Edge Hill, where there was a vast marshalling yard serving the busy docks traffic. Today the yard has gone to make way for Wavertree Technology Park. When the Wavertree Road trams, 4, 4A and 4W, were withdrawn on 15th September 1949, there was a shortage of buses, so the 4A continued to be operated by trams until 11th of December following, but without a route number. (N.N.Forbes)

61. Another view of an unnumbered 4A in Picton Road shows it about to go under the Liverpool-London railway, with the Gem Laundry and the Magnet Cinema left. This is car 342, one of the modernised Priestly cars which along with 343, a sister car, was fitted with a bow collector for a pre-war experiment. (N.N.Forbes)

62. Picton Clock was a focal point on the system where routes 4, 4A, 4W, 5, 42, 48 and 49 merged. English electric car 766, with bogies and controller contactor equipment similar to the Streamliners, has just come from the city as a 4 via Wavertree Road, Picton Road and High Street and has turned into Church Road to stop at the palatious tram shelter. Its indicators are already in position for a return to the city as a 5 via Penny Lane and Smithdown Road. (E.A.Gahan)

63. At the foot of Church Road just before the Penny Lane terminus was Prince Alfred Road tram depot. There was a main entrance off Church Road and a back entrance via Prince Alfred Road itself. Here car 359, pushing its trolley, runs in at the end of peak hour to the back entrance. (N.N.Forbes)

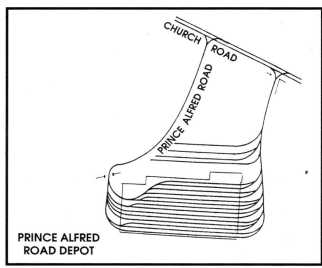

PRINCE ALFRED
ROAD DEPOT

64. Priestly Long Bodied car 753 pauses at Penny Lane on the 4W from Woolton to the City, looking up Church Road (right). This tram, along with car 746, was fitted with Maley & Taunton swing link bogies in July and September 1936 respectively, and both ran as bogie cars until December 1936 (746) and April 1937 (753). Bogie Streamliners 941 and 942, when built, received the bogies and equipment from these two cars, which then reverted to four wheelers, being fitted with EMB Flexible Axle trucks. (S.Watkins)

PICTON CLOCK (WAVERTREE)
TO CHILDWALL FIVE WAYS

65. Car 754 of 1928 is pictured travelling inwards on a 4A at Wavertree Village Green with its ancient lock-up (left). One of the all-conquering new buses overtakes on the 79 route that was to absorb the Childwall Five Ways trams. (E.A.Gahan)

66. With Picton Clock towering above, Baby Grand car 264 is seen on a murky day during the two month period in late 1949 when 4A trams had a lease of extended life and ran numberless. High Street is to the right, citywards. (R.B.Parr)

FARES ON JOURNEYS
TO AND FROM DEPOTS

Childwall Five Ways—Prince
Alfred Road.

STAGE No.   STAGE No.

IN 1½d. FARE (WORKMEN'S RETURN 2d.) OUT
8 Childwall Five Ways and Prince Alfred Road 6

67. Childwall Five Ways terminus was situated at the end of the reserved tracks in Childwall Road. A further extension, which was never officially planned, would have taken trams down Childwall Valley Road to Belle Vale and Lee Park council estates which were not fully developed until after the war. Instead the 79 bus overlapped the 4A and guaranteed it a bleak future. To the left is Queens Drive to the Rocket and north Liverpool. To the right Queens Drive and South Liverpool, and Childwall Priory Road for Woolton. (Merseyside Tramway Preservation Society)

CITY TO PENNY LANE (VIA SMITHDOWN ROAD)

68. Liverpool's celebrity tram 544 is depicted again, this time in pre-war years at the Pier Head, on the then 5 service to Smithdown Road. An obviously super summer's day explains why the top deck windows are lowered right down. (R.B.Parr)

70. Near the Pier Head shelter was an informative route display board that listed all destinations from the terminal. Car 880 on the 5 and car 874 on the 4, join a Priestly wide vestibuled tram on the 1. The two Streamliners are virtually new, whilst the older car is reconditioned and fitted with large indicators. (G.H.F.Atkins)

←

69. The year is 1937, and seen at the Pier Head is Streamliner car 884, with car 276. It was soon to be renumbered 329, to make way for new Baby Grands, and was later lost in the Green Lane fire of 1947. Car 884 later was sold to Glasgow becoming their 1053. The Pier Head once boasted an ornate shelter which unfortunately didn't last through the war. (A.C.Noon Coll.)

Routes 5, 5A, 5W.
WOOLTON—SMITHDOWN ROAD—CITY.

STAGE No.		STAGE No.
(1½d. FARES (WORKMEN'S RETURN 2d.)		
IN		OUT
4	Woolton and Yewtree Road	10
5	Hillfoot Road and Cromptons Lane	9
6	Yewtree Road and Penny Lane	8
7	Cromptons Lane (5W) or Wavertree Clock Tower (5) and Sefton Park Station... ...	7
8	Penny Lane and Portman Road	6
9	Sefton Park Station and Lodge Lane	5
10	Portman Road and Princes Road	4
11	Lodge Lane and Hope Street	3
12	Princes Road and Renshaw Street (Upper Newington)	2
13	Renshaw Street (Upper Newington) and City Terminus	1
2½d. FARES (WORKMEN'S RETURN 4d.)		
4	Woolton and Penny Lane	8
5	Hillfoot Road (5W) or Durning Road (5) and Sefton Park Station	7
6	Yewtree Road (5W) or Ashfield (5) and Portman Road	6
7	Cromptons Lane (5W) or Wavertree Clock Tower (5) and Lodge Lane	5
8	Penny Lane and Princes Road	4
9	Sefton Park Station and Hope Street	3
10	Portman Road and Renshaw Street (Upper Newington)	2
11	Lodge Lane and City Terminus	1
3d. FARES (WORKMEN'S RETURN 5d.)		
4	Woolton and Lodge Lane	5
10	Portman Road and City Terminus	1
4d. FARES (WORKMEN'S RETURN 6d.)		
1	Woolton and City Terminus	1
OUT 2	Durning Road and Princes Road (via Church Road)	3

71. Cabin car 801 is seen in 1937 in front of the Cunard Building at the Pier Head. Route 8 operated only as far as Allerton at this time. Car 801 is in the 1934 livery, but without the upswept streamlined ends, which were discontinued on the first repaint. (R.B.Parr)

72. Bellamy car 248, on route 7 Penny Lane-Pier Head with journeys also to Calderstones, is seen in Dale Street at Castle Street with Exchange Street East to the left. Note also the splendid pose of a police officer on point duty. (R.B.Parr)

73. English Electric balcony car 618 is depicted during the last years of the Second World War on route 5, at what used to be known as Preesons Row, near the Victoria Monument. Left is Fenwick Street. To the right is the former Midland Bank (now Trials Hotel) with a poster exhorting people to buy Defence Bonds. Built by English Electric in 1919, only four of the class (609-633) survived after 1938, and carried the green livery. Car 618 was one of these and ran in service until May 1948. (J.W.Gahan)

Routes 8, 8A.
GARSTON—ALLERTON—CITY.

STAGE No.		STAGE No.
IN	**1¼d. FARES (WORKMEN'S RETURN 2d.)**	**OUT**
—	Dock Road and Danefield Road	11
4	Garston Tram Terminus and Booker Avenue..	10
5	Danefield Road and Greenhill Road	9
6	Booker Avenue and Penny Lane ...	8
7	Greenhill Road and Sefton Park Station ...	7
8	Penny Lane and Portman Road ...	6
9	Sefton Park Station and Lodge Lane ...	5
10	Portman Road and Myrtle Street ...	4
11	Lodge Lane and Hope Street	3
12	Myrtle Street and Mount Pleasant (Upper Newington)	2
13	Mount Pleasant (Upper Newington) and Pier Head	1
	2¼d. FARES (WORKMEN'S RETURN 4d.)	
—	Mersey Road and Danefield Road ...	11
—	Beechwood Road and Booker Avenue ...	10
—	Dock Road and Greenhill Road	9
4	Garston and Penny Lane	8
5	Danefield Road and Sefton Park Station ...	7
6	Booker Avenue and Portman Road	6
7	Greenhill Road and Lodge Lane	5
8	Penny Lane and Myrtle Street...	4
9	Sefton Park Station and Hope Street ...	3
10	Portman Road and Mount Pleasant (Upper Newington)	2
11	Lodge Lane and Pier Head	1
	3d. FARES (WORKMEN'S RETURN 5d.)	
4	Garston Tram Terminus and Lodge Lane ...	5
10	Portman Road and Pier Head	1
OUT	**4d. FARES (WORKMEN'S RETURN 6d.)**	
2 **IN**	Lark Lane and Sefton Park Station	3
1	Garston Tram Terminus and Pier Head ...	

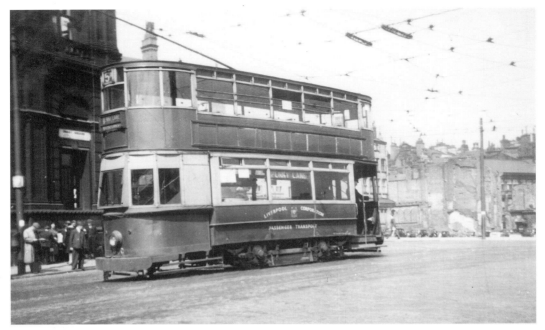

74. Derby Square/Victoria Monument is pictured in the immediate postwar period and Priestly ex-double staircase car 600 stands ready to descend Lord Street past the bomb damaged St George's Crescent, now renamed Derby Square. Car 600 sports the pre-fab windscreen and matches the general decrepitude of the period. (E.A.Gahan)

LIVERPOOL CORPORATION
PASSENGER TRANSPORT

"BUFFER BOYS" - BE WARNED!

ONLY DUFFERS
RIDE ON BUFFERS!
DON'T
DO THIS FOR SPORT AND
BE CRIPPLED FOR SPORT-
FOR LIFE!

75. Car 958 on route 8 and car 162, complete with pre-war advertisements, on route 14 arrive at the top of Lord Street in 1947. Both cars are still in the pre-war livery with dirty cream roofs. Bombed sites, a legacy from the war are in evidence. Both trams look worse for wear having survived the war with minimal maintenance. (R.J.S.Wiseman).

76. Maley & Taunton car 926 descends to the bottom of Ranelagh Street on the day before the Coronation of Elizabeth II, 1st June 1953, the reason the flags are flying. Central station was the Cheshire Lines Committee's terminal until nationalisation in 1948. A Vauxhall pauses at the zebra crossing for a pedestrian, while shoppers are abroad in numbers. (H.B.Priestley)

77. Priestly Long Standard car 756 of 1927 is seen when new at Parker Street/ Clayton Square outside the Owen Owen store. At this time there was an ample tram shelter with a siding where trams could load either side. Car 756 is on the 5A to Calderstones. (J.H.Roberts)

78. Ranelagh Place was a focal point on the system where the Renshaw Street/Mount Pleasant/Brownlow Hill/Lime Street and Ranelagh Street tracks merged. In this August 1937 view, Priestly Wide Vestibule car 321 is on route 1 bound for the Pier Head, whilst Streamliner car 883 is on route 5W for Woolton via Renshaw Street. Route 8 trams would leave via Mount Pleasant, but when route 5, 5W was abandoned, the 8 was rerouted via Renshaw Street allowing the tracks in Mount Pleasant and Oxford Street to be abandoned. To the left is Lewis's Store and, in the background are the splendid buildings which were gutted in the 1941 Blitz. (H.B.Priestley)

79. This is the same spot twelve years later; on the left we glimpse the derelict Lewis's and in the rear is the yawning expanse of the bombed sites. By now, route 8 trams are using Renshaw Street, as depicted here by Maley & Taunton car 918. (R.G.Hemshall)

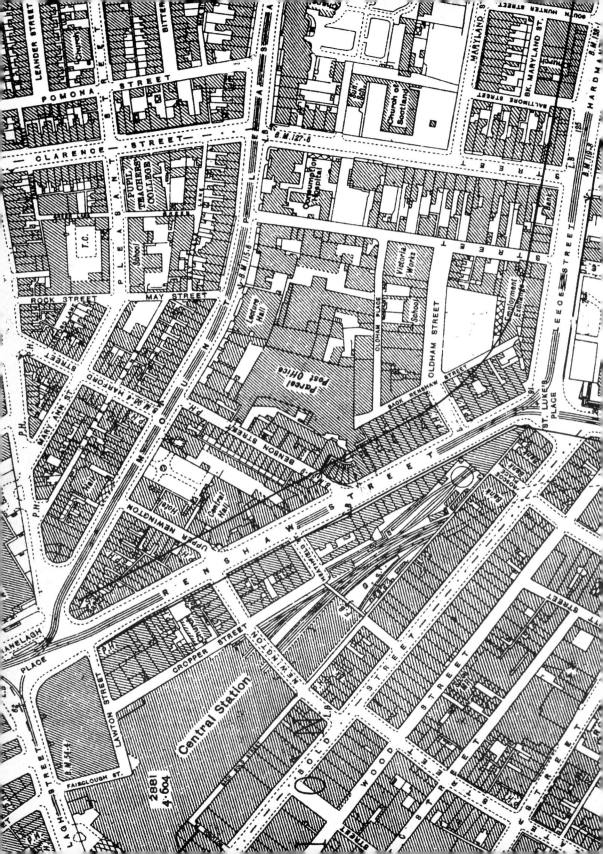

80. Priestly Standard car 719 with non-prefab windscreen pauses at the foot of Leece Street (pronounced locally as Lee-cee) outside what used to be called the Labour Exchange, now demolished. There was a steady slope from here up to the Royal Philharmonic Hall at Hardman Street where it levelled out into Myrtle Street. The tram is on route 5 to Penny Lane and has received a welcome rehabilitation and repaint and for the period it is in excellent condition. (A.C.Noon Coll.)

81. From Myrtle Street tracks curved into Catharine Street to end up at the Rialto junction, where tracks from four directions merged. Here car 746 is seen at the Rialto just entering the Georgian splendour of Upper Parliament Street. The tracks in the foreground were used by route 25 from Princes Road into Upper Paliament Street. Car 746 was a long Priestly vestibuled car built in 1927, rebuilt in 1937 with ventilators, transverse seating and new EMB Flex trucks and along with car 753 experimentally sported Maley & Taunton bogies for several months. (A.C.Noon Coll.)

82. Further along Upper Parliament Street car 884 has just crossed the Grove Street junction and is travelling citywards. Since the 1980s riots and the subsequent demolition and landscaping, the thoroughfare has decidedly lost some of its Georgian character. This picture was taken on 1st June 1952. (R.J.S.Wiseman)

→

83. A scene which has completely changed is this view of Smithdown Lane/Smithdown Road/ Lodge Lane/Tunnel Road and Earle Road junction. The only building extant is the distinctively domed Martins Bank, no longer a bank. The street to the left is a short length of Smithdown Lane from which Upper Parliament Street curved citywards. Modern road management and property demolition renders this location practically unrecognisable from our scene of car 883 on an 8A bound for Garston on the day before the Coronation, 1st June 1953. (R.J.S.Wiseman)

→

84. Smithdown Road sloped from Tunnel Road then levelled out by the hospital and cemetery and our shot of Bellamy car 365 is at Brookdale Road. The tram is on the 4/5 belt route - 5 outwards to Penny Lane, then change indicators to 4 for a return to the city via Wavertree. Our conductor has been a bit premature in changing his indicators to 4! Model train and tram fans will know this spot for Hattons Model Railway emporium. (B.P.Martin Coll.)

85. Wartime blackout necessitated white painted tree trunks and poles and white buffers on car 659 on route 5 as it picks up passengers in Smithdown Road by Dudley Road. Note one of the illuminated stop signs which fell into disuse during the war and behind the tram, the power station and Smithdown Road car shed opened in 1899 and closed to trams in 1936, when Prince Alfred Road became the main tram depot. (N.N.Forbes)

87. Route 7 to Penny Lane was somewhat overtaken by the extensions to Woolton and Allerton, which left this route a mere adjunct to these other south end trunk routes. Originally City to Penny Lane with extensions to the popular Calderstones Park (part way on the Woolton route), it later became peak hours only and mainly the preserve of older handbraked cars in their twilight years. This surprising view is of car 954, a practically new Streamliner, at Penny Lane on the 7 was taken in about 1938. (T.A.Packwood Coll.)

86. Penny Lane, one of the hubs of the tramway system where cars to Garston (1, 8) and Woolton (4W, 5W) met cross-city routes 46 and 49 and cars on the 4/5 belt. With Heathfield Road and Church Road behind, Maley & Taunton car 931 pauses on belt route 5 with a Baby Grand on a 49 about to go round the turning circle to return to Muirhead Avenue East via Church Road. (Merseyside Tramway Preservation Society)

Route 7.
PENNY LANE—LONDON ROAD—CITY.

STAGE No.		STAGE No.
IN	1½d. FARES (WORKMEN'S RETURN 2d.)	OUT
8	Penny Lane and Portman Road	6
9	Sefton Park Station and Lodge Lane	5
10	Portman Road and Myrtle Street	4
11	Lodge Lane and Crown Street...	3
12	Myrtle Street and Lime Street	2
13	Lime Street and Castle Street	1
	2½d. FARES (WORKMEN'S RETURN 4d.)	
8	Penny Lane and Myrtle Street... ...	4
9	Sefton Park Station and Crown Street	3
10	Portman Road and Lime Street	2
11	Lodge Lane and Castle Street	1
	3d. FARE (WORKMEN'S RETURN 5d.)	
10	Portman Road and Castle Street	1
	4d. FARE (WORKMEN'S RETURN 6d.)	
1	Penny Lane and Castle Street	

88. A Maley on the 8 on the main line at Penny Lane is travelling towards the city, Smithdown Road is ahead, with Allerton Road behind with to the right, in the middle of the loop, "the shelter in the middle of the roundabout" later immortalised in the Beatles song "Penny Lane". A former tram shelter it latterly became Sgt. Pepper's Bistro! St Barnabas Church is on the left, whilst the actual Penny Lane itself goes off to the left (H.B.Priestley)

PENNY LANE TO WOOLTON (VIA CALDERSTONES)

89. Allerton Road is the location as Maley car 926 leaves Penny Lane for Woolton on the 5W. In the 1950s there were ample grassed islands giving shoppers refuge from the traffic. With the demise of trams and the proliferation of the motor car the road was widened and the grass verges discontinued. (Merseyside Tramway Preservation Society)

90. Today this important junction of Queens Drive/Allerton Road and Menlove Avenue is known as the "Allerton Maze". In the 1970s and 1980s traffic management schemes resulted in double roundabouts and a combination with traffic lights. In tram days it was a simple junction of the 4W and 5W trams to Woolton to the left, and 1, 8 trams to Garston, right. Here a Woolton bound Streamliner heads outwards along Menlove Avenue. The absence of road traffic is remarkable. (E.A.Gahan Coll.)

91. Green Lane/Menlove Avenue was photographed in 1920 as car 523, a Bellamy in First Class livery, heads citywards on a 4A to the city from Calderstones. Along this section the finials took the form of Liver Birds, Liverpool's mythical motif. The extension to Woolton was completed in 1924 which resulted in the unusual and only example of the suffix W (for Woolton) being used, hence the 4W and 5W route numbering. (B.P.Martin Coll.)

92. The tracks to Woolton were on reservation once past Calderstones/Cromptons Lane. Here car 869 heads citywards at this point as it traverses Cromptons Lane crossover. In early days when Calderstones was an important terminal serving the nearby public park, there was also a lengthy loop. The tram in the picture is now preserved and operating at the National Tramway Museum in Crich, Derbyshire. It was sold to Glasgow in 1954, becoming Glasgow Corporation car 1055. It was bought for preservation in 1960. (Merseyside Tramway Preservation Society)

93. One stop beyond Calderstones, modernised car 342 halts at the Yew Tree Road/Beaconsfield Road intersection on its way to Woolton on service 4W. The distinctive Liverpool lighting brackets on the tram poles are clearly evident as are the end of reserved track bollards with their distinctive illumination. (E.A.Gahan Coll.)

94. Further along the reserved tracks towards Woolton was the Vale Road stop. A Baby Grand heading outwards and a war-grimed Priestly standard provide the service in this 1949 scene. (N.N.Forbes)

→

95. At the end of the superb Menlove Avenue reservation, the Woolton route turned at the Derby Arms into Allerton Road (Woolton) and then to the terminal in High Street. Trams held sway, no other traffic is in sight and as yet there is no property development. At first 4A and 5A route numbers were used until the suffix W was deemed more obvious to the possibly confused prospective passengers. (B.P.Martin Coll.)

→

96. Twenty five years on in May 1949 and Baby Grand car 274 has just entered the reserved tracks in Allerton Road (Woolton). The scene has not changed here over the years since tram days. To the right is Camp Hill and Woolton Woods, a popular destination of generations of small boys utilising their penny returns! On the left is a row of splendid cottages built with sandstone hewn from Woolton's own quarry in nearby Quarry Street. (Wallasey Tramcar Preservation Group)

TRANSFER FACILITIES

AVAILABLE ON TRAMCARS ONLY

The Transfer System operates in order to enable passengers to travel from point to point by alternative routes at the same fare as exists on the through routes. Use of the Transfer Facility obviates long waits for through cars in the City area, gives a wider choice of vehicles and avoids the necessity of walking to the terminal points in the City. Generally, the journey must be in the direction of the through route, although exceptions have been made in cases where a through route does not exist, and a link-up permitted with cross-city routes.

THE TRANSFER MUST BE MADE AT A RECOGNISED TRANSFER POINT BY THE FIRST AVAILABLE CAR IN THE REQUIRED DIRECTION.

97. For the last few stops before reaching the High Street terminus, the trams completed their journey on reserved tracks. Here Priestly Standard car 20 has just passed Quarry Street and the world famous hosiery factory of Bear Brand. The year is 1949 - the last year of trams to Woolton - car 20 survived for just 14 months more before being scrapped. (N.N.Forbes)

———————▶

98. Car 942 is made ready for departure for the city from Woolton terminus. The conductor takes a breather after no doubt utilising the bundy clock. The ecclesiastical buildings are the Woolton Methodist Sunday Schools and St James Methodist Chapel in Church Road. (N.N.Forbes)

———————▶

99. The first green liveried cars were the Priestly Bogie cars 770-781 which appeared in 1933. Popular at the time was film star George Arliss whose latest offering was a jungle epic entitled "The Green Goddess". Naturally the nickname was applied to the 770 class, and to every new Liverpool tram that subsequently entered service! Car 772 is seen at Woolton after being driven out for a series of publicity photographs on its launch. The title on the rocker panels was "Liverpool Corporation Tramways" which was changed to "Passenger Transport" with the first Streamliners in 1936. (Liverpool Corporation Passenger Transport)

100. An interior series of pictures was also taken at Woolton. The top deck shows the modern concealed lighting, upholstered seats with ample grab knobs, vestibule on the stairs to stop any extraneous draughts, all in an environment which provided clear forward vision. This was a huge step forward in Liverpool tram design compared with what had gone before in the shape of Priestly's earlier offerings. (LCPT)

101. The lower saloon had concealed lighting, transverse seats, veneered panelling and a bright outlook. A startling departure compared with the earlier more traditional trams. (LCPT)

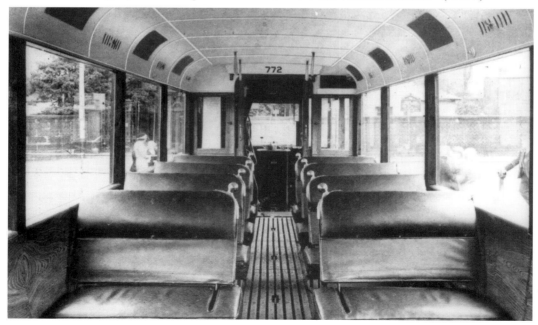

PENNY LANE TO GARSTON (VIA ALLERTON)

102. Route 8 trams to Garston shared tracks with Woolton cars for the short length from Penny Lane to Queens Drive. Marks Bogie car 819 on the 8 to Garston follows a Streamliner on the 4W to Woolton at Plattsville Road. The spacious pavements were soon lost in road widening here when buses replaced the Woolton trams. The Marks Bogie series (818-867) were mounted on either EMB HR/2 radial arm bogies or EMB Lightweight bogies, except for odd man out car 819 which received Blackpool pattern English Electric bogies from the beginning. (S. Watkins)

Liverpool Corporation Passenger Transport

ALLERTON TRAMWAY EXTENSION

Commencing Tuesday, 4th July, 1939

Route No. 8—PIER HEAD—ALLERTON

and

Route No. 46—WALTON—PENNY LANE

will be

EXTENDED TO GARSTON
Via Island Road South

Also A CIRCULAR SERVICE

WILL BE INTRODUCED BY LINKING UP AT GARSTON

Route No. 8—GARSTON—ALLERTON—PIER HEAD
(above)

with

Routes Nos. 1 & 45-GARSTON-AIGBURTH-PIER HEAD

For particulars of Time Tables, Routes and Fares—see over.

CENTRAL OFFICES,
24 HATTON GARDEN,
LIVERPOOL 3.
June, 1939.

W. G. MARKS, M. INST. T.,
GENERAL MANAGER.

B.& H. Ltd. 4945 (30,000)

103. Looking towards Penny Lane, car 878 is about to cross Queens Drive and has just passed Limedale Road/Emsworth Road in the days before road widening. Expansive landscaped verges with their attendant trees certainly made the area attractive. The picture was taken on Monday, 8th June 1953, two days after the last trams to Garston. Car 878 is seen being transferred from Garston Depot to Walton Depot for further service in the city. This car was one of the second batch of 22 that was sold to Glasgow in 1954, becoming Glasgow car 1041, being finally withdrawn in April 1959. (R.J.S.Wiseman)

104. Streamliner car 972 is pictured in Allerton Road at Hillside Road stop, again showing the attractive landscaping along this section. It is last tram week on the Garston Circle and the tram has the road to itself. (R.Anderson)

105. Mather Avenue, that splendid "straighter than an arrow" tram reservation, became home ground to the new Streamliners. A fairly new car 870 is photographed from the top deck front seat of sister car 165 at Greenhill Road in September 1939 as the threat of war results in white painted kerbs. (S.Watkins)

106. "Fine trams on fast tracks" was the motto of the service on the Garston route along Mather Avenue. Maley car 937 passes Greenhill Road on its journey into the city. (R.Stephens)

107. Car 878 on route 1 is depicted travelling to Garston and its onwards journey via Aigburth to the Pier Head. It has just left its lone passenger at the Cleveley Road stop with the square tower of All Souls, Springwood, rising in the mist in the distance. The Police Training College is on the right. (J.H.Roberts/WTPG)

108. Rounding the curve from Allerton Station, Maley car 922 opens up on the Mather Avenue reservation towards the tram stop at Danefield Road. (R.Stephens)

109. The Danefield Road stop on Mather Avenue with All Souls Church in the background, is seen as car 966 on an 8A to Garston only draws away after depositing several passengers during the last week of trams to Garston. (R.Anderson)

110. Number indicator already turned to 33 for its journey around the Garston circle via Aigburth to the city, car 878, a regular Garston depot car, is seen passing Danefield Terrace Apartments near Longcroft Avenue. The tram is sporting the new style number indicators with much narrower characters. (R.Stephens)

111. Viewed from Allerton Station overbridge on the Liverpool to London line with Woolton Road (right) and Stamfordham Drive (left), a Streamliner on route 33 advances towards the bridge approach tracks about to dip under the station. Not much road traffic is apparent save for a parked Morris 8 and a Standard. The date is 22nd April 1952. (H.B.Priestley)

112. This is Woolton Road, looking towards Allerton Station with the crossover and siding for South Liverpool Football Club whose Holly Park ground is on the right. A feeder (right) supplies the power to the overhead wires as Maley car 936 heads for the city via Mather Avenue. (H.B.Priestley)

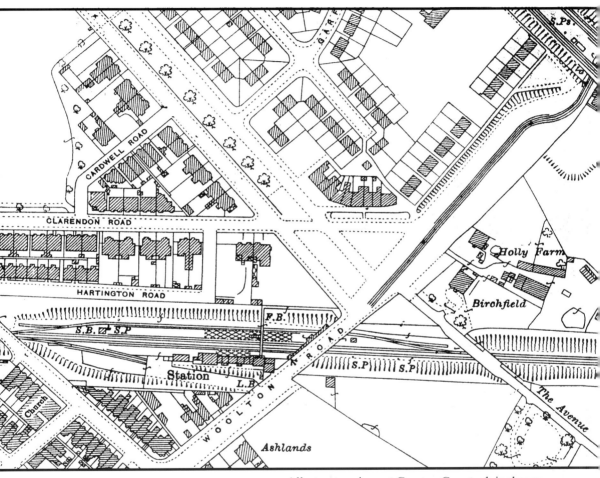

113. Allerton was photographed on the last Friday of the route, 5th June 1953, and car 932 on the 33 passes over the Cheshire Lines railway with the cenotaph in the background on the Long Lane triangle. To the right in the distance can be seen the former LMS Allerton Station overbridge. (R.J.S.Wiseman)

Allerton terminus at Garston Cenotaph is shown before the construction of Horrocks Avenue and the extension and link up with Garston to form the Garston circle. Allerton station is top right and Garston station is on the left.

114. In July 1939 the Horrocks Avenue link was completed, enabling trams to continue from Allerton through to Garston. To maximise the new tracks, a circular service was inaugurated linking Allerton, Garston and Aighburth with the city. Routes 1 and 8 were originally linked, then on the demise of the 1, routes 8 and 33 formed the Garston Circle. In the immediate postwar period property development ensued with dwellings and a school built on the right. To the left was the popular Garston Market. (W.J.Wyse)

TRANSFER SYSTEM to and from City Termini

CITY TERMINI: Pier Head.   South Castle St.   Old Haymarket.   North John St.   Lime Street.
               London Road.   Gt. Crosshall St.   Moss Street.   Commutation Row.   Castle Street.

Direct Route.		TRANSFER ALTERNATIVES: Transfer Point.		Fare
1, 1A, 33, 45	Garston via Dingle	20, 21, 25	...Dingle (Ullet Road) 1, 1A, 33, 45	
		20, 21, 25	...Aigburth Vale 1, 1A, 33, 45	
4, 4A, 4W	Wavertree Clock Tower	5, 5A, 5W, 7, 8, 8A, 32, 46	...Penny Lane ... ...4, 4W, 49...	
		6, 6A, 40	...Mill Lane, Edge Lane Drive...49	
4A	Childwall	4, 4W	...Wavertree Clock Tower ...4A	
4W 5W	Woolton	4, 4A ...	...Wavertree Clock Tower ...4W	
4, 4W, 5, 5A, 5W, 7, 8, 32	Penny Lane	4, 5, 5A, 7, 8, 8A, 32, 46	...Penny Lane 4W, 5W	
		4A	...Wavertree Clock Tower ...4, 4W, 49	4d.
6, 6A	Mill Lane, Edge Lane Dr.	4, 4A, 4W	...Wavertree Clock Tower ...49...	
6A	Bowring Park	6, 40 ...	...Edge Lane Dr., Broagd'n Rd. 6A	
		6	...Broadgreen Station ...6A	
8, 8A	Garston via Allerton	4, 4W, 5, 5W, 7, 32, 46	...Penny Lane 8, 8A	
9, 10	Old Swan	11, 12, 29, 29A	...Green Lane, West Derby Rd. 49	
10A, 10B 10C		11	...Green Lane, Prescot Rd. ...9, 10, 10A, 10B, 10C, 49 ...	

115. Turning from Speke Road, car 928 enters the Horrocks Avenue reserved tracks on the penultimate day of tram operation, 5th June 1953. Because of the war and the subsequent change of policy, the tramway extension to Speke did not take place. This would have gone off to the right towards the airport. (R.J.S.Wiseman)

116. The furthest point south on the Garston Circle was the terminus in Speke Road. The depot is on the left. Here car 667, a Priestly Standard with pre-fab windscreens departs for the Pier Head via Mather Avenue in 1947. On the left the Speke bound 82 bus provides a service that the trams would have done but for the hostilities. (R.B.Parr)

PEAK HOUR ROUTES 32 AND 38

117. Peak hour route 32 operated from Penny Lane to Castle Street via the "back way" into the city along Park Lane, thus avoiding the shopping streets of Church Street, Clayton Square and Renshaw Street and their attendant congestion. In 1946 Priestly Balcony car 314 is still in the old red and cream livery with rocker panel in red; a top deck enclosed green car 61, also bound for Penny Lane, follows. A good rule of thumb for viewing black and white pictures concerning Liverpool trams is that trams in the red livery wore their fleet numbers above the headlight and all green cars had them below. Today the Victoria Monument is on a pedestrianised plaza fronting the Queen Elizabeth II Law Courts. (N.N.Forbes)

118. Postwar peak hour service 38 linked Penny Lane with the docks at Seaforth. Pre-war tram services 37 and 38, the Wavertree belt, based on Old Haymarket gave way in 1941 to short workings on the 4 and 5. Pictured is Bellamy car 555 on one of the 37/38 belt services, about to travel to Old Haymarket via Smithdown Road. The Bethel Welsh Presbyterian Church forms an imposing backdrop to Penny Lane loop with car 645 on a 5A and a new Streamliner on the 4W. (A.C.Noon Coll.)

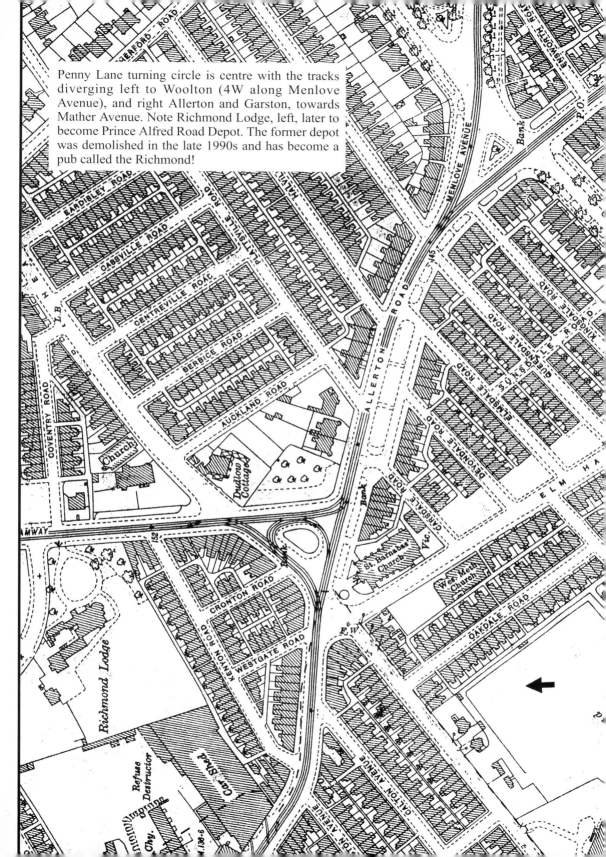

Penny Lane turning circle is centre with the tracks diverging left to Woolton (4W along Menlove Avenue), and right Allerton and Garston, towards Mather Avenue. Note Richmond Lodge, left, later to become Prince Alfred Road Depot. The former depot was demolished in the late 1990s and has become a pub called the Richmond!

SOUTH END FINALE

119. The night of Saturday, 6th June 1953, saw the finale of trams in the south end of Liverpool. Hundreds gathered at Garston to welcome car 979 (pictured), the last on route 8, and the last 33, which was car 967. Driver Trembath and Conductor Hodgson somehow are not sharing the smiles and jollity of the locals. (South Liverpool Weekly News)

LIVERPOOL CORPORATION PASSENGER **TRANSPORT**

TRAM ROUTES

GARSTON **8, 33** PIERHEAD

CONVERSION TO BUS OPERATION AND RENUMBERING 86 & 87

COMMENCING

SUNDAY, 7th JUNE, 1953

Routes and Fares unchanged

Pier Head Terminus transferred to front of Liver Building

Minor adjustments will be necessary to other stops

Workmen's Returns, Transfers and Children's Holiday Returns will not be available on buses

Details of revised Route Numbers on back

| 24 Hatton Garden, Liverpool 3. | 'Phone CENtral 7411 | W. M Hall, General Manager |

Garston terminus and depot in 1927. Horrocks Avenue is not yet built.

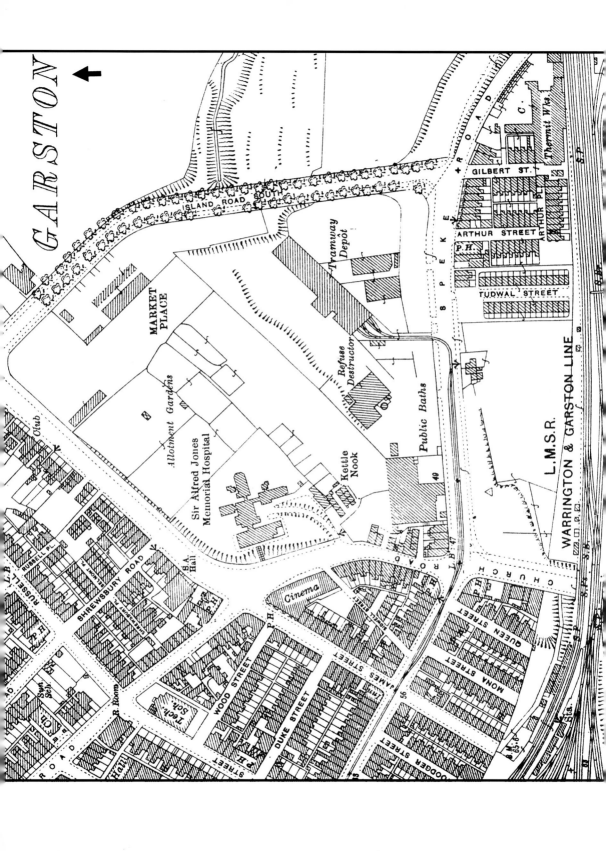

GARSTON

ISLAND ROAD SOUTH

MARKET PLACE

Allotment Gardens

Sir Alfred Jones Memorial Hospital

Club

RUSSELL PL.

SHREWSBURY ROAD

R. Room

RUSSELL P

Sun Sch.

Tech. Sch.

B.A. Hall

Cinema

WOOD STREET

DUKE STREET

JAMES STREET

STREET

DODGER STREET

Tramway Depôt

Refuse Destructor

Kettle Nook

Public Baths

S P E K E   R O A D

CHURCH

QUEEN STREET

MONA STREET

GILBERT ST.

ARTHUR STREET

ARTHUR

P.H.

TUDWAL STREET

Thermit Wks.

C.

P.H.

L.M.S.R.

WARRINGTON & GARSTON LINE

P.H.

P.H.

ROLLING STOCK

BELLAMY CARS.....1-4, 134-140, 142-441, 442-483, 484-570, 573-576.

Liverpool began its first years of electrification by experimenting with different trams. The fact that the imported German Altona, Ringbahn and American Philadelphia types were unsuitable to Liverpool's conditions made the Corporation seek a design that would exactly match the needs for the new burgeoning city wide network of routes.

Originally built with three window saloons and open tops, the Bellamys saw various developments until the final form of a solid timber roof and fully glazed upper saloon extending over a shorter lower saloon.

Cars 1-5 were oddments built in 1907 used to fill gaps in the fleet numbering, but the Liverpool Standard trams 142-441 (1900), built by Dick, Kerr, were turned out at an incredibly fast rate to meet the demands. Originally open top they were soon top covered, first by canvas blinds, then with glazing and finally they acquired the characteristically solid Bellamy roof. Cars 442-483 were a continuation - all cars to 471 appeared new with top covers with opening roof sections and pull down canvas blinds. From car 472 examples were then built at the Corporation's own Lambeth Road Works. They were constructed with glazed upper saloon windows, however, some later received an extended canopy over the balconies. Cars 484-570 were the final series, the ultimate development of 1907, of which the First Class cars were mostly picked from this series. Cars 573-576 were the last development of this ubiquitous class, the last two having extended canopies.

Known as Bellamy cars after C. R. Bellamy, the General Manager, they evolved over 14 years from 1899 to 1913. The famous "Preston" car developed for Liverpool was

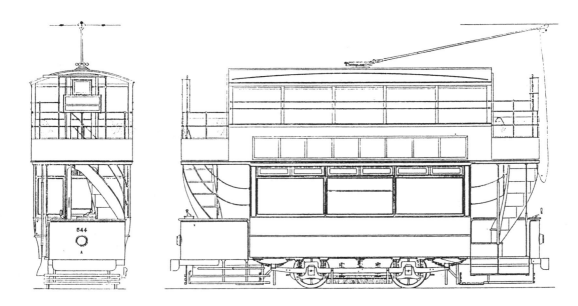

adopted widely as tramway electrification gathered momentum countrywide. Many tramway representatives visited Preston and ordered cars of the type they saw being built for Liverpool. Altogether Dick, Kerr built 330 cars for the city before the Corporation began to build its own cars at Lambeth Road.

C.W.Mallins succeeded Bellamy as general manager in 1906, and added Manchester type canopies to some cars. Some of the last batch, cars 535, 543 and 544, were fitted with wide bodies enabling tranverse 2+2 seating in the lower saloon. By 1913 the class totalled 446. By 1933 scrapping began in earnest with the influx of new Priestly types entering service. In 1934 only 272 survived but in declining condition, some were now over 30 years old. The disposal reads: 15

rebuilt to balcony type in 1921/22, 86 rebuilt to Priestly type in 1922/23, 21 converted for departmental use in 1941/43, and the rest, a total of 323 were scrapped between 1934 and 1938, except of course for car 544 which survived in service until 1949. Car 558 was rescued for preservation in 1951, but was unfortunately disposed of in 1954 after open storage in a builder's yard at Kirkby.

The Bellamys were to be found all over the Liverpool system, but car 544 endeared itself to staff and tram enthusiasts alike by surviving for so long. It was shedded at Prince Alfred Road Depot and could be seen on south end duties including trips to Muirhead Avenue East and the East Lancashire Road to Kirkby on the 48 and 49.

120. Three Bellamys are seen in August 1937. On the right is 484, which was a first class car from May 1911 until April 1923; it was built in 1907 and withdrawn in March 1940. The middle car has been fitted with a balcony top cover; this is 350, which was built in 1901 and ran until July 1938. The car at the back of the line is 437, built in 1901 and withdrawn in April 1938. These three cars had not long to exist, soon to be replaced by new Streamliners. The two archtypal Bellamys are in the late 1930s style of simplified livery, with the rocker panel in maroon. The original condition is shown by the middle car, which retained its "Liverpool Corporation Tramways" legend. (H.B.Priestley)

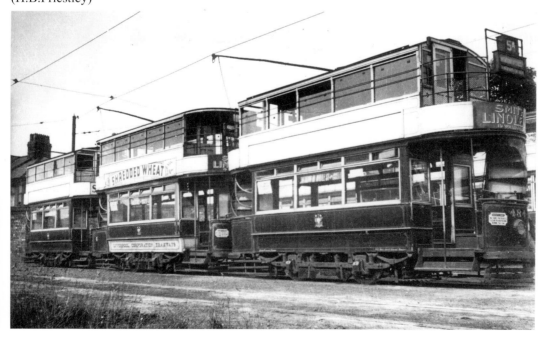

MALEY & TAUNTON STREAMLINERS....
918-942

The Bogie Streamliners were numbered 868-992 and 151-188, variously fitted with EMB Lightweight and EMB HR/2 radial arm bogies, but the series of 25 cars numbered 918-942 received Maley & Taunton swing link bogies from their inception in 1936/37. Two sets of Maley equipment had already been fitted to cars 746 and 753 with the intention of using the other 23 sets to modernise the rest of the long bodied Priestly cars. However, it was decided to equip new Streamliner bodies with these 23 trucks. The last two cars of the series, 941 and 942, were then fitted with the bogies from cars 746 and 753, which in turn reverted to EMB flex trucks.

When new, this class was to be found on the Prescot Road route, but then spent most of its life shedded at Prince Alfred Road, before transferring en bloc to Garston where passengers on the Garston Circle were then provided with a fast service by modern cars.

The Maley & Taunton bogies had swing links, fixed bolsters and outside axle hung motors. The bogie wheelbase was 4ft 6in/1372mm, some 3 ins/76mm shorter than the EMBs. The weight of the bogie was carried on the side pads, the load being transmitted directly to a big inverted leaf spring just behind the side frame and thence to coil springs. There was virtually no bolster, because the centre pivot carried no weight. Road clearance was limited and encounters with projecting granite setts were often destructive. This allowed their use only on routes with good trackwork and smooth paving. As the Garston Circle tracks were in good order, it made sense to utilise these 25 non-standard Streamliners.

They all survived the war remaining in service until car 920 was withdrawn in January 1953 with supposedly defective bodywork.

However, the remaining 24 were surplus to requirements in June 1953 with the closure of the Garston Circle and Garston Depot.

After a short while in store at Edge Lane Works, the overture to Glasgow bore fruit. The Scottish city agreed to purchase the 24 Maleys. They later purchased a further 22 cars the following year. Car 942 was the first to enter service in Glasgow in October 1953 as Glasgow car 1006.

The Glasgow numbers were:

918-1022	927-1024	935-1009
919-1030	928-1013	936-1021
921-1016	929-1029	937-1020
922-1018	930-1010	938-1008
923-1012	931-1011	939-1023
924-1027	932-1014	940-1015
925-1025	933-1028	941-1026
926-1019	934-1007	942-1006

On arrival in Glasgow all cars of this class had to be regauged from Liverpool's standard 1435mm track gauge to Glasgow's 1416mm. In Glasgow they lost their buffers due to clearance difficulties of the Glasgow loading gauge and they eventually received small windows in the top deck front window for ease of reversing the bow-collectors which replaced the Liverpool trolleys. New interior concealed lighting was fitted and with the livery of green, cream and orange certainly the Maleys wore a disguise for the native Liverpudlian. However, Glasgow found them not to their liking and abhorred their propensity for water ingress. In order to remedy this situation, Sylglas tape was applied in an attempt to stem the water; unfortunately the "patched up" cars had a most unattractive appearance. New one-piece driver's windscreens and non-streamlined D windows also contributed to a detrimental appearance. Only entering service in October 1953, they were gradually withdrawn between 1958 and 1960.

121. Liverpool Maley & Taunton Bogie Streamliner car 940 is pictured in its Glasgow guise, running as GCT car 1015. It is on service 15, Anderston Cross to Baillieston in August 1957. It retains so far its Liverpool windscreen, but has not yet been fitted with resistance ventilators (under the stairs), nor has it been fitted with replacement non-streamlined shaped D windows. (B.P.Martin)

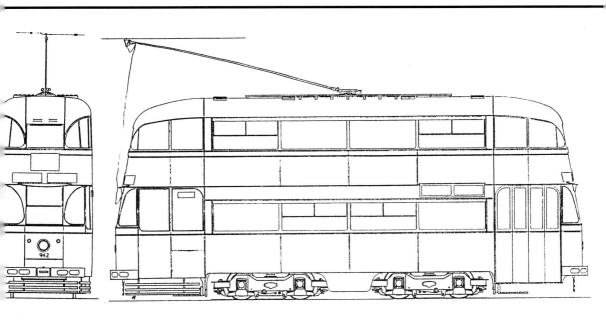

MP Middleton Press

Easebourne Lane, Midhurst, West Sussex. GU29 9AZ Tel: 01730 813169 Fax: 01730 812601
...WRITE OR PHONE FOR OUR LATEST LIST...

BRANCH LINES
Branch Line to Allhallows
Branch Lines to Alton
Branch Lines around Ascot
Branch Line to Ashburton
Branch Lines around Bodmin
Branch Line to Bude
Branch Lines around Canterbury
Branch Line to Cheddar
Branch Lines to East Grinstead
Branch Lines to Effingham Junction
Branch Line to Fairford
Branch Line to Hawkhurst
Branch Line to Hayling
Branch Lines to Horsham
Branch Line to Ilfracombe
Branch Line to Kingswear
Branch Lines to Launceston & Princetown
Branch Lines to Longmoor
Branch Line to Looe
Branch Line to Lyme Regis
Branch Lines around Midhurst
Branch Line to Minehead
Branch Lines to Newport (IOW)
Branch Line to Padstow
Branch Lines around Plymouth
Branch Lines to Seaton & Sidmouth
Branch Line to Selsey
Branch Lines around Sheerness
Branch Line to Tenterden
Branch Line to Torrington
Branch Line to Tunbridge Wells
Branch Line to Upwell
Branch Lines around Wimborne
Branch Lines around Wisbech

NARROW GAUGE BRANCH LINES
Branch Line to Lynton
Branch Lines around Portmadoc 1923-46
Branch Lines around Porthmadog 1954-94
Branch Line to Southwold
Two-Foot Gauge Survivors

SOUTH COAST RAILWAYS
Ashford to Dover
Brighton to Eastbourne
Chichester to Portsmouth
Dover to Ramsgate
Hastings to Ashford
Portsmouth to Southampton
Ryde to Ventnor
Worthing to Chichester

SOUTHERN MAIN LINES
Bromley South to Rochester
Charing Cross to Orpington
Crawley to Littlehampton
Dartford to Sittingbourne
East Croydon to Three Bridges
Epsom to Horsham
Exeter to Barnstaple
Exeter to Tavistock
Faversham to Dover
Haywards Heath to Seaford
London Bridge to East Croydon
Orpington to Tonbridge
Swanley to Ashford
Tavistock to Plymouth
Victoria to East Croydon
Waterloo to Windsor

Waterloo to Woking
Woking to Portsmouth
Woking to Southampton
Yeovil to Exeter

EASTERN MAIN LINES
Fenchurch Street to Barking

COUNTRY RAILWAY ROUTES
Andover to Southampton
Bournemouth to Evercreech Jn.
Burnham to Evercreech Junction
Croydon to East Grinstead
Didcot to Winchester
Fareham to Salisbury
Frome to Bristol
Guildford to Redhill
Porthmadog to Blaenau
Reading to Basingstoke
Reading to Guildford
Redhill to Ashford
Salisbury to Westbury
Strood to Paddock Wood
Taunton to Barnstaple
Wenford Bridge to Fowey
Westbury to Bath
Woking to Alton
Yeovil to Dorchester

GREAT RAILWAY ERAS
Ashford from Steam to Eurostar
Clapham Junction 50 years of change
Festiniog in the Fifties
Festiniog in the Sixties
Isle of Wight Lines 50 years of change
Railways to Victory 1944-46

LONDON SUBURBAN RAILWAYS
Caterham and Tattenham Corner
Charing Cross to Dartford
Clapham Jn. to Beckenham Jn.
Crystal Palace and Catford Loop
East London Line
Finsbury Park to Alexandra Palace
Holborn Viaduct to Lewisham
Kingston and Hounslow Loops
Lewisham to Dartford
Lines around Wimbledon
London Bridge to Addiscombe
North London Line
South London Line
West Croydon to Epsom
West London Line
Willesden Junction to Richmond
Wimbledon to Epsom

STEAM PHOTOGRAPHERS
O.J.Morris's Southern Railways 1919-59

STEAMING THROUGH
Steaming through Cornwall
Steaming through East Sussex
Steaming through the Isle of Wight
Steaming through Kent
Steaming through West Hants
Steaming through West Sussex

TRAMWAY CLASSICS
Aldgate & Stepney Tramways
Barnet & Finchley Tramways
Bath Tramways

Bournemouth & Poole Tramways
Brighton's Tramways
Bristol's Tramways
Camberwell & W.Norwood Tramways
Clapham & Streatham Tramways
Dover's Tramways
East Ham & West Ham Tramways
Edgware and Willesden Tramways
Eltham & Woolwich Tramways
Embankment & Waterloo Tramways
Enfield & Wood Green Tramways
Exeter & Taunton Tramways
Gosport & Horndean Tramways
Greenwich & Dartford Tramways
Hampstead & Highgate Tramways
Hastings Tramways
Holborn & Finsbury Tramways
Ilford & Barking Tramways
Kingston & Wimbledon Tramways
Lewisham & Catford Tramways
Liverpool Tramways 1. Eastern Routes
Liverpool Tramways 2. Southern Routes
Maidstone & Chatham Tramways
North Kent Tramways
Portsmouth's Tramways
Reading Tramways
Seaton & Eastbourne Tramways
Southampton Tramways
Southend-on-sea Tramways
Southwark & Deptford Tramways
Stamford Hill Tramways
Thanet's Tramways
Victoria & Lambeth Tramways
Waltham Cross & Edmonton Tramway
Walthamstow & Leyton Tramways
Wandsworth & Battersea Tramways

TROLLEYBUS CLASSICS
Croydon Trolleybuses
Bournemouth Trolleybuses
Maidstone Trolleybuses
Reading Trolleybuses
Woolwich & Dartford Trolleybuses

WATERWAY ALBUMS
Kent and East Sussex Waterways
London's Lost Route to the Sea
London to Portsmouth Waterway
Surrey Waterways
West Sussex Waterways

MILITARY BOOKS
Battle over Sussex 1940
Blitz over Sussex 1941-42
Bombers over Sussex 1943-45
Bognor at War
Military Defence of West Sussex
Secret Sussex Resistance

OTHER BOOKS
Betwixt Petersfield & Midhurst
Brickmaking in Sussex
Changing Midhurst
Garraway Father & Son
Index to all Stations
South Eastern & Chatham Railways
London Chatham & Dover Railway

SOUTHERN RAILWAY VIDEO
War on the Line